SPECTACULAR SPIDERS

written by Lori C. Froeb
reviewed by Louis N. Sorkin, B.C.E.

Reader's Digest
Children's Books®

Pleasantville, New York • Montréal, Québec • Bath, United Kingdom

What Is a Spider?

Eight legs, eight eyes, sharp fangs. This may sound like a description of an alien from outer space, but these creatures are all around you. They are spiders, and there are about 40,000 different **species** of them!

Spiders are **arachnids**, and they are related to scorpions, ticks, and mites. Instead of having three body segments, like insects, they have two: a **cephalothorax** and an abdomen. All eight legs are connected to the cephalothorax and many of the organs are in the abdomen. Most spiders have eight eyes, but some have six, four, two, or no eyes at all. Tarantulas can be as large as dinner plates, while some tropical spiders are as small as pinheads.

Did You Know?

This daddy longlegs might look like a spider, but it's not! Also called a harvestman, this leggy creature has what appears to be only one body segment, unlike spiders which have two.

No matter what their size, all spiders are predators. All spiders have fangs—and some can inject a deadly poison into their victims. Spiders eat mainly insects, but some big species can kill and eat scorpions, lizards, small mammals, and even birds.

Marbled Orb Weaver

What's That Word?

As you read, you will see words that are in **bold** type. Look for them in the glossary on page 22 to learn what they mean.

Spiders, Inside-Out

What's inside a spider's compact body? Lots of the same things that you'd find in yours! Spiders have a brain, a heart, muscles, a stomach, and even a special kind of lung.

A spider's organs do the same things yours do. The brain and nerve cord control all of the body's movements and functions. The heart pumps blood to all the organs. The stomach breaks food down into nutrients for the body to use. Food is first drawn into the sucking stomach, then it moves into the midgut (similar to your intestines).

Spiders—like insects, mammals, birds, and fish— need oxygen in order to live. Air filters through a pair of organs called **book lungs** in the abdomen. Once inside the body, oxygen seeps into the blood. Some spiders have one pair of book lungs, while others have two.

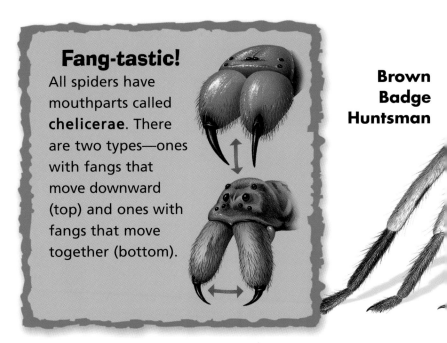

Fang-tastic!

All spiders have mouthparts called **chelicerae**. There are two types—ones with fangs that move downward (top) and ones with fangs that move together (bottom).

Brown Badge Huntsman

Also in the abdomen are organs called spinnerets. Located near the spider's behind, these organs squirt silk. Other **arthropods** make silk, but only spiders produce it in every life stage.

Eye Spy

Wolf spiders like this one have eight eyes—two large eyes and six smaller ones. Because this spider actively hunts its food, it has very good eyesight and also has an amazing sense of touch.

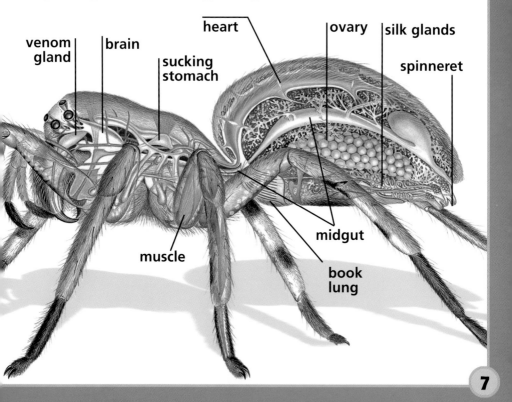

venom gland

brain

sucking stomach

heart

ovary

silk glands

spinneret

muscle

midgut

book lung

Body Language

Spiders have the same needs as all other living creatures: to find food, to find a mate, and to keep from being eaten. Their senses help them do all these things. A spider sees through a group of eyes along the front of its cephalothorax. In certain spiders, such as jumping spiders, the middle pair of eyes focus on an image, while the rest of the eyes notice even the smallest movement. Many spiders can't see well and depend on body hairs to "see" and sense the world. Some hairs sense movement—on the ground, in the air, or on the water's surface. Other hairs—especially on the **pedipalps** and legs—are used to smell and to taste.

Spiders use their sense organs to communicate with each other, too. Male wolf spiders dance to attract females. Several kinds of spiders coat their silk in **pheromones** to send special scent messages to others of their species. Some use vibrations to talk to possible mates by tapping messages on their webs with their legs or pedipalps.

This male jumping spider is trying to get a female's attention by showing off his colors and patterns in a special dance. If the female is interested, they will mate.

Friend, Not Food!

The male black widow spider (right) is much smaller than the female. He must be careful when walking on her web. She might think he's food! He taps a message on the silk to let her know he'd like to mate.

Spider Cycle

It's a rough world out there for spider babies, but most spider moms do their best to give their young a good start. All spiders lay eggs—there may be only a few eggs or thousands of them—and wrap them in a silk sac. This keeps the eggs protected and safe from **parasites**. Many mothers carry this sac with them until the eggs are ready to hatch; other mothers protect the sac in webs or burrows. Some females die soon after laying their eggs. These spiders simply camouflage their sacs and leave them hidden from enemies.

Once the **spiderlings** have hatched, they huddle together. After a few days, they leave the nest. If they didn't separate, they'd eat each other! They may simply crawl to new homes or "balloon" to new areas. To balloon, a young spider points its abdomen into the air and lets out a strand of silk. The wind catches the silk and carries the spider away. Spiders can travel quite far this way.

Growing Pains

In order to grow, spiders must **molt** their **exoskeletons**. Depending on the species, a spider may molt up to 30 times during its life. After leaving its old exoskeleton, a spider's body is very soft. It must stay hidden until its new exoskeleton hardens.

A wolf-spider mom carries all her newly hatched spiderlings on her back. Special hairs on her abdomen help them get a good grip. There may be as many as 200 spiderlings riding piggyback!

This nursery-web spider carries her egg sac with her everywhere she goes. Just before the eggs hatch, she builds a special nursery by wrapping silk around the stems and leaves of a plant. Then she stands guard to protect her family from enemies.

Sensational Silk

One of the most interesting things about spiders is their ability to make silk. Silk is made in special glands in the spider's abdomen and is almost as strong as steel of the same thickness. It's also very stretchy. Scientists have learned that there are seven different kinds of silk. Each is good for a specific purpose—wrapping prey or eggs, lining burrows, making trip wires, and, of course, web building.

Most spiders that build webs are trying to catch prey. The webs are hard to see and are made from sticky strands. Insects that fly into the web stay put while the hungry spider rushes out to wrap its prey in silk for safekeeping. Funnel-web spiders build tube-shaped webs on the ground. When the spider feels the vibrations of a passing insect on its web, it attacks. Other spiders don't make webs at all because they hunt their prey.

Did You Know?

Silk is liquid until it hits air. The spider pulls the liquid silk out of spigots on the spinnerets. Several strands come out at once, and the spinnerets work like fingers to weave the strands together into a sheet, band, or thread.

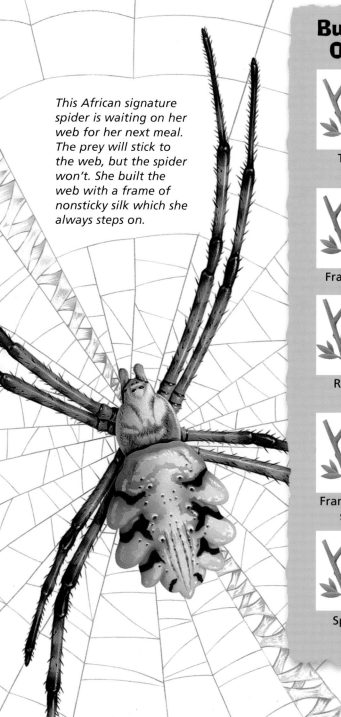

This African signature spider is waiting on her web for her next meal. The prey will stick to the web, but the spider won't. She built the web with a frame of nonsticky silk which she always steps on.

Building an Orb Web

The first fork

Frame completed

Radial threads attached

Frame spiral of dry silk in place

Spiral of sticky silk added

Hunters and Ambushers

All spiders are meat eaters, but the ways they catch their food varies from species to species. Most spiders trap prey, but about 18,000 species hunt their food or wait for something to **ambush**.

Most hunting spiders eat beetles, ants, or even other spiders. But some big spiders—like tarantulas and huntsmen—can grab and kill frogs, lizards, small rodents, or birds. Many spiders have a hunting territory. Wolf spiders will chase off any other spiders that try to move in on their hunting grounds. Jumping spiders have amazing eyesight and can see an insect eight inches away. They attack by leaping onto their prey.

Spiders that ambush rely on not being seen. The trapdoor spider hides in its nest underground. When it senses prey nearby, it flips open its camouflaged "trapdoor" and grabs lunch. Crab spiders can change colors to blend in with the flowers they hunt on—surprising flies and bees.

Did You Know?

People once thought that wolf spiders hunted in packs and worked together to catch prey—as wolves do. That is how these amazing hunters got their name.

Gone Fishing

Fishing spiders will hold on to land or plants with their back legs and dangle their front legs on the water's surface. When they feel vibrations of passing prey, they dive into the water to grab it!

Mexican red-kneed tarantulas have very poor eyesight and use organs on their legs to pick up vibrations from prey. They attack fast with fangs that are almost half an inch long!

Time to Eat!

Spiders are webmasters, and when it comes to dinner, they have other ingenious ways of using silk. Diving-bell spiders build dining rooms out of silk underneath the water. Once the room is constructed, the spider fills it with air from the water's surface. The spider leaves to hunt and brings dinner home to be eaten in the air pocket. Some spiders make traplines that hang from simple webs. The lines are stretched onto the ground and have sticky ends. When an insect walks onto a trapline, it snaps back, with the victim dangling in the air.

Once a spider gets its prey, it has an interesting way of eating. A spider can't swallow solid pieces of food. Instead, it **paralyzes** its victim with venom and then vomits in strong juices that turn the insides of its prey to liquid. This makes it easy for the spider to suck it up through its small mouth. Almost all spiders must eat this way.

Dangling for Dinner

Bolas spiders like this one eat only one kind of insect—armyworm moths. The spiders attract the moths with a female moth scent. When a male moth flies by, the bolas spider swings a silk thread that has a sticky glob on the end. It sticks onto the moth, and the spider reels it in!

Dinner to Go

After paralyzing her grasshopper prey with a fast bite, this spider quickly wraps it in bands of thick silk. Once her catch is wrapped, the spider can store it until she is ready to eat it.

This ogre-faced spider hangs from a branch and waits for an insect to crawl by. When it spots one with its super-large eyes, the spider throws a small elastic web—like a fishing net—over its prey to trap it.

Staying Off the Menu

What's to worry about when you are a spider? Getting eaten! Birds are probably the biggest threat, but lizards, toads, small mammals, and even other spiders also enjoy spiders for lunch.

How do spiders stay alive? That depends on the spider. Some simply stay out of sight when they aren't hunting. Others will suddenly drop from their webs if approached, hoping their attacker won't spot them dangling below. Many spiders use camouflage to blend in with their surroundings or **mimic** other more dangerous animals, like wasps. The South African white lady spider curls its legs under its body and quickly rolls down sand and dunes to escape trouble.

Some spiders—like spiny orb weavers—make such painful mouthfuls that birds don't bother. Tarantulas can flick barbed hairs at attackers, sending even larger enemies running.

Did You Know?

Female green lynx spiders are very protective of their egg sacs. If a predator gets too close, she will spit powerful venom from her fangs. She can spit as far as eight inches!

Don't Touch!

No one likes to eat poop. That's why this spider is safe out in the open— even during the day. Her body is colored and shaped like a pile of bird droppings, keeping her hidden from even the hungriest predator.

When a predator, like this giant centipede, barges into a trapdoor spider's burrow, the spider runs into its secret room and pulls the door shut. Not finding the spider, the centipede eventually leaves.

Super Spider Facts

As you've read, spiders are amazing creatures. Although many people dislike spiders, we'd be in trouble without them. A spider can eat up to 2,000 creatures in its lifetime—many are pests like cockroaches, scorpions, or other spiders that are dangerous or annoying to humans. Right now there are 2 billion insects for every human on Earth. Without spiders to help control their numbers, we'd be swimming in a sea of insects!

Want to learn more about our eight-legged friends? Help yourself to these amazing spider facts!

Spider comes from the Old English word *spinnan*, which means "to spin."

Many spiders will shed a leg to get away from an attacker. There is no limit to how many legs spiders can lose—as long as they can still eat. Lost legs can grow back with the next molt—as long as the spider is not an adult already.

Ogre-faced spiders have two gigantic eyes that are hundreds of times more sensitive to light than a human's. Ogre-faced spiders can see prey in almost total darkness.

After a volcanic eruption, all life was wiped out on the island of Krakatoa. Just a few months later, scientists noticed the first new inhabitants: spiders that had ballooned there from 25 miles away!

Some tarantulas can live to be up to 30 years old.

Black widow venom is 15 times more poisonous than rattlesnake venom. Only a very small amount is injected, so very few people die from it.

Some of the largest webs in the world are spun by orb-weaving spiders in New Guinea. Their webs can be up to nine feet across and are strong enough to be used as fishing nets.

Glossary

ambush: An ambush is a surprise attack. When a spider ambushes prey, it hides until its victim gets close, then quickly grabs it.

arachnid: A creature that has eight jointed legs and two body segments, but has no antennae or wings. Spiders, mites, ticks, and scorpions belong to this group.

arthropod: An animal with joined legs and an exoskeleton. This group of animals includes insects, spiders, crabs, scorpions, centipedes, millipedes, ticks, and mites.

book lung: A book lung is used for breathing. It is made of many flat sheets, like the pages of a book. This helps the spider get lots of oxygen.

cephalothorax: Instead of a separate head and thorax, spiders have a cepaholothorax that includes both.

chelicerae: A spider's mouthparts, used for grabbing and sometimes crushing prey. Each chelicera has a sharp fang that can inject venom into prey.

exoskeleton: This word comes from the Greek words *exo*, which means "outside" and *skeletos*, which means "dried up" or "hard." An insect's exoskeleton is made of many pieces that are joined with a softer material that helps it bend.

mimic: A creature that copies or acts like another animal is a mimic. Spiders fool attackers into thinking they are dangerous or poisonous animals when they are not. This keeps them from being eaten.

molt: The process spiders, insects, and other arthropods use to grow. When a creature molts, it sheds the outer layer (or exoskeleton) of its body.

paralyze: When something is paralyzed, it can't move. Most spiders have a paralyzing venom that keeps their prey from struggling while being eaten.

parasite: A plant or animal that lives or feeds off another plant or animal (called a host). Usually the parasite doesn't kill its host, but makes it very sick.

pedipalp: A spider has two pedipalps near its mouth. They are used to touch, taste, and smell.

pheromone: A pheromone is a scent used by some animals to communicate with others of its species. Pheromones attract mates or warn others of danger.

species: A group of living things (plants or animals) that have enough things in common to be able to reproduce.

spiderling: Baby spiders right after they hatch from eggs.